T0197129

Intentional Living and Leadership

Consciousness, Choice and Planning for Success

Craig C. Sroda

authorHOUSE®

AuthorHouse™
1663 Liberty Drive
Bloomington, IN 47403
www.authorhouse.com
Phone: 1 (800) 839-8640

Published by AuthorHouse 07/28/2015

ISBN: 978-1-5049-2488-7 (sc)
ISBN: 978-1-5049-2487-0 (e)

Library of Congress Control Number: 2015911952

Print information available on the last page.

This book is printed on acid-free paper.

Contents

Introduction

Intentional living—the conscious choice to create your life, to respond rather than react, to chart your own course both professionally and personally—is an amazing thing. However, it's also difficult to achieve.

Life should be more than a series of situations in which you find yourself. It should be more than a string of events in which you are a passive observer, or someone who takes a reactionary stance. Intentional living requires that you act, that you decide, that you *choose.*

Living intentionally can be tough though. You must know yourself—both your internal and external selves. You must know your blind spots, which can be impossible to do without outside help. You must build your life and live according to your core strengths, but what are they? How do you learn about them?

These are just a few of the questions I've faced. I've struggled to answer them. I co-founded a company and became a CEO by the age of twenty-eight. I've since learned that success isn't found in the boardroom or in business accomplishments or even in raising amazing children and seeing them grow. In fact I've come to believe that success isn't a thing at all—it's something much more.

Having a life plan is vital, but charting a course into the unknown future can be daunting if you don't know who you are, what you stand for, and don't have the support of a strong foundation. You must prioritize all areas of your life, and learn to lead—not fearlessly but with humility and emotional intelligence.

These are the lessons I've learned so far in life—and each new day brings another opportunity for learning and personal and professional growth.

Chapter 1

Strengths and Weaknesses

Knowing your strengths and weaknesses is absolutely essential. While I've read a number of books that discuss the topic, one of the first was *Now, Discover Your Strengths* by Marcus Buckingham. It's stayed with me through the years, and it opened my eyes to the reality that each of us has five core strengths—and we have to focus on them.

Your Five Major Strengths

Each of us has five major strengths. The sooner you know what they are, the better off you'll be. Both my wife and I have been long-term strengths advocates, not just for our three daughters, but also for their friends and extended family members as well.

While the book I mentioned above was instrumental in developing my understanding of our five core strengths, there was another that played a significant role: *Strength Finders 2.0* by Tom Rath. It is an excellent book, and I can't tell you how many copies we've purchased and given away over the years.

Knowing your strengths is vital for achieving success, and that knowledge plays a central role in your decision-making, including the career you choose. I've heard uncounted stories of doctors becoming doctors because their parents were, then being so incredibly unhappy with their lives that they flat-out quit. Tradition is all fine and good, but if a career choice doesn't speak to your five core strengths there is simply no way that you'll ever find it rewarding in the long term.

When you finally do capitalize on your strengths, you'll be a happier person—both consciously and unconsciously. You'll have a more positive impact on the world and those around you, and you'll see significantly greater success.

When I discuss these ideas with others—whether my girls, their friends, or someone else—they're pretty receptive, but I go about it in a specific way. I've found that it helps to make them more open and to eliminate potential distractions. It's usually something along these lines:

1. Get them out of the house or office, as the case may be.
2. Give them the book with the code for online access. My wife and I try to write something personal to each recipient inside the cover.
3. Open my laptop and create an account for them.
4. Let them answer the questions. It takes about twenty minutes.
5. Feed them. This goes a long way toward creating an atmosphere conducive to conversation and learning.

6. Review their five core strengths with them.
7. Review the action plan, and print it out, or email it to their account. Email is generally easier, particularly if you're doing this on the run.
8. Have them add a contact to their phone's address book for Strengths Finders along with their name.

It's amazing to see the big picture materialize in their minds. I feel that it changes the trajectory of who they'll become down the road. Of course, the goal here is to give them the information necessary to make smart, informed, accurate decisions in life.

Now, I've been doing this for some time. I started with my wife and myself and then my three daughters, but I didn't really put it into practice during my early learning. However, it's become a constant guidepost now. As the younger generation matures, their understanding of those strengths will guide them during decision-making. It's all about giving them information about themselves so they can make better decisions in all aspects of their lives from choosing college majors to taking a job.

Identifying Your Five Core Strengths: Take Action

First, you really should pick up *Strength Finders 2.0*. While there are plenty of similar tests out there, this one is simple, easy, and accurate. It also works with any age group. Once you've got the book, take the assessment with a family member. You can also try it with your coworkers.

After eighteen years of serving as CEO at Pinnacle, and my time as CSO, I need to keep not only *my* strengths but those of others in mind at all times. During my last two hiring sessions, I spoke openly about my personal and professional weaknesses and told each of them that they would have to offset those weaknesses. It was honest and direct, and it told them exactly what to expect in the position. It was an incredible way to build a firm foundation.

Blind Spots

Blind spots exist in both your personal and professional life. In fact, we require outside validation from someone else on what we see and think in thirty percent of our lives. There's simply no getting around it—it's an unchangeable part of being human. The trick is to ensure that you have someone you trust checking your blind spots—someone who can hold you accountable.

I was out with a colleague once—a successful businessman. He defined success as having run a growing business for a number of years, building the bottom line, and having the material things he wanted in life. For me, success is different: it's having a life filled with purpose. It's striving for balance. It's prioritizing the right things and giving in proportion to taking. I value time more than I ever have before. It's really the only thing you own.

During my meeting, I asked my colleague a few questions. I think you'll find his answers enlightening in terms of blind spots and the need for a trusted ally.

I asked, "Who is keeping you accountable?"

His reply? "No one."

Not satisfied, I pressed him further. "Do you have a group that you hang in of which you're the dumbest member?"

He gave me a strange look, but the answer was the same: "No."

I decided to press further. "Do you listen to any podcasts, read blogs, listen to audiobooks, or read books?" The only answer I needed was the expression on his face.

For the executive or head of a company it's important to have someone exposing your blind spots and helping advise you on business, technology, and life-balance (because if life-balance is out of whack, you'll just burn out). Your life-accountability partner might be someone else, but someone should be there for you.

I decided to pull together a list of books, blogs, and podcasts that would be helpful for my colleague, who has since become a friend. I've listed those books below and provided the links for easy downloading.

It's essential to expose your blind spots so you have a different viewpoint on both business and personal matters. For your personal life this might be a friend or life-coach. For business it might be a board of directors or a technology committee. It might be a steering committee, a leadership team, or even a business coach.

Whatever you do though, actively strive to always have someone to expose your blind spots. It could even come from one of the books, blogs, podcasts, and audiobooks I've included below. It could be an accountability partner or someone else. Remember: you grow out of your comfort zone, and it will be uncomfortable.

I like to cite these quotes to my daughters:

- The purpose of life is a life of purpose.
- You don't plan to fail; you fail to plan.
- Leaders read, and readers lead.
- Realization of your life moving from success to significance is a life- and maturity-thing. Embrace it, and the sooner you get to significance the better your life will be. No ego allowed.

If you'd prefer a PDF of the links I've included below, you can download one here: Craig Reference Guide v1.

Craig's Reference for Growth and Blind Spot Exposure

What (Who)	Type	Focus	Link
EntreLeadership (Dave Ramsey)	Podcast	Business and life	Subscribe with your podcast app
This is Your Life (Michael Hyatt)	Podcast	Leadership	Subscribe with your podcast app
Your Move (Andy Stanley)	Podcast	Faith and life	Subscribe with your podcast app
EntreLeadership	Blog		Subscribe/Read
This is Your Life	Blog		Subscribe/Read
Seth Godin	Blog		Subscribe/Read
Create Your Life Plan (Michael Hyatt)	eBook	Life planning to determine priorities	http://michaelhyatt.com/life-plan
Good to Great (Jim Collins)	Book/ Audiobook	Business foundation and culture	Good to Great
Great by Choice (Jim Collins)	Book/ Audiobook	Business foundation and attitude	Great by Choice
The Advantage (Patrick Lencioni)	Book/ Audiobook	Business leadership and teams	The Advantage
Tribes (Seth Godin)	Book/ Audiobook	Marketing genius	Tribes
The Rockefeller Habits (Verne Harnish)	Book/ Audiobook	Business strategy and team building	The Rockefeller Habits
How Great Leaders Inspire Action (Simon Sinek)	TED Talks Online Speaker		Sinek TE

In What Group Are You the Stupidest Member?

Let's take a moment to explore a concept I mentioned above. When speaking to my colleague, I asked him if he was involved with any group in which he was the stupidest member. It sounds odd, but let's consider this. It's kind of crazy, but the fact is that we grow when we're out of our comfort zone. The logical question then is, when are you out of that zone?

We all have groups that we hang out with ranging from our family to friends, coworkers, colleagues, extended family, and more. There has to be a group in which you are not the leader, where you're not the dominant force or primary intellect. In this group, you're the one who stays quiet—who listens rather than leads.

In this group, you're uncomfortable because you don't have all the answers and you have little influence, if any. Most people don't like to feel dumb or be the lowest on the totem pole, but if you don't have this type of group, it's a huge problem.

Don't mistake me. It's okay to lead in many groups, but you cannot lead in all of them. That means you're not learning from others, and learning is more valuable than leading. I ran a technology company for eighteen years, and I love being a leader that builds other leaders, but being humble around other leaders greater than you is something that should always be in your playbook.

Do You Always Lead?

Write down the groups in which you're a member. Mark out the ones in which you're the leader. Count the groups where you feel uncomfortable or dumb. If you don't have at least one, find one immediately and enjoy the experience of learning and humbling yourself.

Craig C. Sroda

Stretching: Comfort Zone or Strengths Zone?

I ran the Indianapolis Mini-Marathon with my daughter, relatives, and a few friends once. It was a real accomplishment, and I was euphoric to finish the 13.1 miles in just 2.08 hours.

As a "forever learner," I always strive to stretch myself and expand my comfort zone. One of the most important things I do in life is to have "red flags." Red flags are activities I perform to ensure I'm not going off track. Think of them as mile markers or guideposts. One big red flag is running a race each year. I used to have ten kilometer races as the mark, but a few years back I upped that to half-marathons. The idea here is that the flags alert me that I'm not matching my lifestyle to my goals and growing into who I want to become. A perfect example is running the half-marathon.

If I can't finish the race, it means I'm doing something in my life that's preventing me from reaching that goal. The alert might be that I'm drinking too much or not getting enough sleep. Maybe I'm not getting enough exercise. Based on that flag, I adjust my lifestyle to ensure that I can achieve my lifetime goals.

Another goal I set was to do more public speaking—definitely something that would expand my comfort zone. Once I led a technology whiteboard discussion with the Renaissance Executive Forums CFO peer group. Exciting and highly interactive, it encouraged me to go to the next level, where I had the opportunity to speak at the Chief Executive Boards International Summit in Atlanta on the topic of business strategy and technology alignment. The audience was made up of about fifty-five CEOs and owners, which really pushed me out of my comfort zone. I prepared, read the book *Talk Like TED*, and things went better than I'd anticipated.

Because of my belief in stretching my comfort zone, I read the book *StandOut* by Marcus Buckingham. He discusses the *comfort zone* versus *strengths zone*, which really forced me to think. He mentions not blindly stretching your comfort zone, as you may end up in someone else's strength zone and lose. That was something I'd never considered.

Some goals do stretch the comfort zone, but with your career you should be strategic in your choices. Focus on your strengths zone. Ultimately it will help you reach that "sweet spot" and help you become a happier, more successful person.

With team members, it's important to get them fully engaged. As a leader, you must take ownership of what you are asking of your team. Remind yourself that you put them where they are for a reason. Make sure you understand their viewpoints, and if they are not in their strengths zone, move them somewhere else. If your team members don't want to understand their strengths or make the needed adjustments, they shouldn't be part of your team. It's a disservice to keep them on board if they aren't performing. Saying that—asking your team what they are working on and how you can help—often opens up good dialog. Building goodwill and helping others just feels good too. Seek to understand, then to be understood.

If you're ready to push your comfort zone and better understand your strengths, create red flags or mile markers in your life that will tell you when you're going off track. I highly recommend reading *StandOut* by Marcus Buckingham too. Remember your strengths and drive into storms to address what needs to be addressed.

Craig C. Sroda

Just Because You Can Doesn't Mean You Should

Just because you can doesn't mean you should—that's something my wife has been telling me for years, although it took some time for it to really sink in. The message definitely applies to both my professional and personal life.

My wife and I grew up without much. Being blessed with three wonderful daughters, I wanted to give them more than we had. Don't all parents? Many people fall into this trap. Yes, it is a trap—even with the best of intentions.

You work hard and want to take away some of the struggle and pain that you had to handle during your own youth. I made plenty of mistakes with my daughters, like getting them computers for their rooms too soon. This resulted in separation from the family and other downsides that go along with technology. Simple conversations were difficult as instant messaging and texting became constant distractions.

I think I heard it on Andy Stanley's podcast. He said, "It's okay to give your kids what you didn't have, as long as you give them what you did have that made you you." That really opened my eyes and correlated directly with what my wife has been saying all along.

I'm incredibly thankful for my wife; she's been a great foundation for our family. She's kept our core values in place and provided great meals to have conversation around, building a consistent foundation and simply being there when our daughters needed to talk. I've always pushed forward, as my strengths are centered around achieving things, strategy, and planning for the future. I wanted to give them more, and my wife wanted to give them a foundation that we lacked growing up.

As you add new things to your life and business, keep a balance between what you have and what you still want. Determine the impact of new items. Anything you add should be balanced with your core values and foundation.

In your personal life, look back and remember the foundational items that made you who you are. Determine if you want those in your life today. If so put a plan in place and start incorporating them into your life. Try to understand the impact of adding technology or things you didn't have, and make sure it doesn't take away the things you had and want to have. Understand your and your spouse's strengths and love tanks, as this will lead to a happier life.

In your professional life, make sure you understand the impact to the business before you put new systems in place. New systems that aren't part of a long-term integrated strategy and only have a short shelf life aren't always wise choices. Remind yourself that money can buy technological improvements, but people make them work. Ensure that you're thinking about all three business components: people, process, and systems.

Remember that training your people is and always will be a great investment, and culture is a very big deal. Make sure you're sharing your vision and why you are doing what you're doing. Create a technology road map that is aligned with your business strategy, and ensure you're getting outside points of view. Blind spots around technology can be especially costly.

Guardrails: Preventing Derailment

I mentioned red flags previously. Now it's time to talk about the concept in greater depth. While listening to Andy Stanley's podcast series about guardrails, I realized the concept he was explaining was the same one I called my "red flags." *Guardrails* is probably the better word.

As life becomes more complicated, there are more devices to pull us off track, and people and situations can stop us from achieving our objectives and goals. The formal definition of a guardrail is, "a system designed to keep vehicles from straying into dangerous or off limit areas." They are designed to keep the damage from being as bad as it could have been, and to create smaller accidents in order to avoid big or fatal ones.

Guardrails are never placed in the danger zone because they're meant to keep us out of that zone. This applies well beyond the road and has significant implications for both your work and personal life. Here's a question—when you did something bad, or something you shouldn't have been doing, were you with a friend? More than likely, the answer is yes. I love Andy Stanley's quote, "Our culture baits us to the edge, but then chastises us when we take the bait. How close are you pushing the limits? If someone you loved were watching, would you do the same activity?"

I use red flags or guardrails to hold myself accountable for goals and objectives like running a half marathon per year, as well as other health goals, family goals, and purpose goals. After listening to Andy's podcast, I realized adding guardrails related to my kids to my life was another worthwhile step.

Do you have guardrails in your own life? Would you be proud of your actions at work and at home if someone you loved and trusted were watching? Be true to yourself at all times. When you fail—and we all do—get up and add another guardrail so it doesn't happen again.

Building Your Guardrails

First, inventory your friends. Are they pulling you in the direction you want to go? Are they pushing your comfort zone in the wrong direction? Evaluate them, and make changes. Do you have enough guardrails in your life? Are you protecting your marriage or other significant relationship? Do you have boundaries with coworkers at work? Are you being the parent or friend that you want to be? Are you taking care of yourself—health, growth, learning, spirituality, balance? Do a life-plan if you can't answer those questions. If you're asking, "Is it a sin to ______?" you're in a danger zone.

Remember that acceptance leads to influence, and it can be dangerous. Live your life as best you can with a conscious, proactive mentality.

Black and White and Shades of Gray

Segueing directly from guardrails, let's talk for a moment about boundaries, and how the world is not really just shades of gray. Have you ever found yourself uncertain due to a lack of boundaries? It's ironic how we test boundaries throughout our life—as kids with parents, as employees with employers, as customers with vendors. Whenever there's an area of gray, it will be tested.

On the other hand black and white is timeless not just in fashion, motorcycles, and newspapers, but in our everyday lives. We need those boundaries. We need black-and-white areas. We need to know where our guardrails are. Goals and measurements have always been part of my life. And yet, both as a parent and in the office, I occasionally fall into the gray zone. Whether it's by choice or accident, it happens.

We once had the opportunity to meet with a new potential customer. Unfortunately many of their internal processes were in shades of gray. Processes that are not clearly defined are left to individual interpretation, and the outcome of that interpretation is difficult to predict. For predictability, black-and-white processes with goals and measures are essential. Similarly, a lack of clear communication in processes means that outcomes are even less predictable.

After taking a long look in the mirror, I realized it's only with clearly-defined black-and-white areas that success is truly predictable and achievable.

Paint It Black (and White)

First, identify those gray areas in your life. Determine which ones should really be black and white, and think about the outcome you want for each area. Determine which areas need tighter guardrails or defined black-and-white rules. Put an alarm in place to alert you when you're in a gray zone, and remember: you don't plan to fail. You fail to plan.

Healthy Conflict

Most of us want to avoid conflict, while a rare few actually thrive on it. Did you know that conflict could actually be healthy? It's hard to believe but true. I was once in a meeting where the tension was palpable. You could cut it with a knife. There were tons of different viewpoints being expressed, and I completely disagreed with a decision direction. I'm passionate about the future by nature, which is definitely one of my five core strengths, so I expressed my differing opinion that the decision would have a negative impact on our future. Despite the tension and conflict, we pushed through to the next topic.

One of the most important concepts I've learned over the years is that conflict is normal in all areas of life. Understanding and practicing the concepts of emotional intelligence—which we'll cover in another section—can help when you must manage tension that so often appears at work, home, and play.

TRUST	FEAR
Safety	Stress
Being Heard	Loss of potential
Openness	Deception
Healthy disagreements	Limitation
Risk-taking	Damaged Relationships
Innovation	Stored resentment
Inspiration	Sabotage
Loyalty	Resigning
HEALTHY CONFLICT	UNHEALTHY CONFLICT

During that high-tension meeting, I struggled with self-regulation because I was angry. I felt I was being misunderstood, and they just weren't getting it. I didn't regulate much, and after reconsidering things that was fine. I didn't attack anyone personally. I simply stated my opinion and spoke the truth.

Managing tension is and will always be part of life. It's fine to have disagreements, differing opinions, and to be passionate or get angry once in a while. Healthy conflict can help an organization grow in many good ways. Proverbs 27:17 states, "As iron sharpens iron, so one person sharpens another." We need to butt heads sometimes to sharpen one another, or increase awareness.

During high-tension situations, remember the following:

1. Remember the goals; ask yourself what you're trying to achieve.
2. State the facts—being honest and upfront helps you reach step #4.
3. Don't get personal—personal attacks only increase conflict and don't move the conversation toward goals.
4. Have open and engaged discussions—you need to feel safe in order to speak openly.
5. Share your emotion on the topic—this allows others to help you work through blind spots.

It's important that when a decision is made, even if it's not yours, you must support it when you walk out of the room. You just have to let go of the emotion, the conflict, and the passion. Throw your support behind it. Don't gossip or spread negativity. One thing that I love about Dave Ramsey is that he has a "zero gossip" policy. He defines gossip as talking to someone that cannot do anything to help with the issue. Gossip is a culture killer, so guard against it.

Kill the Gossip: Taking Action

Kill the gossip in your workplace and personal life. Engage in healthy conflict and support decisions when they're made. Understand the importance of emotional intelligence, and know your strengths. Take the test so you're aware of your five core strengths.

Spend Fifteen Minutes with Yourself

Can you spend fifteen minutes alone with yourself? It doesn't sound like much of a challenge, but according to a study conducted by the *Journal of Science*, sixty-six percent of people can't do it. In fact they gave themselves an electric shock rather than be alone with just their thoughts for that short period of time.

I'm an enormous fan of audiobooks, podcasts, online courses, and pretty much anything else that helps you become a better person. Intentional living according to your values and beliefs must be part of your life. I've used this saying several times during this chapter, but it bears repeating—you don't plan to fail, you fail to plan.

Interestingly, I've written over the concept of owning your own day—I'll cover that later on in this book—and part of that is spending fifteen minutes of quiet time with just your thoughts. Since learning of the study I just mentioned, I've tried to pay closer attention to my thoughts during those fifteen minutes early each morning. It was very cool when I heightened my awareness of where my thoughts were going, and how fast they jumped around. You're either in control of your thoughts—which requires effort—or they control you.

Give it a try yourself. Try fifteen minutes of quiet time. Where does your mind go? Can you be still with just your own thoughts? Would you rather shock yourself to get out of it?

Defining Success and Overcoming Your Lizard Brain

What does success mean to you? A few years back, I was working on my life-plan and the question came up of what I defined as success. It's a tough question. It really depends on where you are in life, and you will find that your definition changes over time, particularly if you lack a strong foundation. My foundation is my faith and my family. Matthew 7:24 speaks of the importance of a solid foundation—are you building on rock or sand?

Understand this—success is always relative. It's not absolute. It means something different for each of us, regardless of the fact that the media and the traditions of our own culture put enormous pressure on people to find "absolute success." It's often defined by money or by achieving a particular point in your professional life.

Success is a continuous process, and it never ends. Once you have achieved a particular goal or goals, you set new ones. You march on. If one of your goals is to have a family of your own, then you'll set a new one once that's been achieved. You'll want to raise your children right, help them get an education, and so on. Success is a state of being, not a final target.

Finally, success should be personal, and no one has the right to tell you what it should be in your case. Of course that means you have to break out of the media-promoted image of money, power, and popularity.

The Lizard Brain

An essential element of attaining success on your own terms is overcoming the lizard brain, that primitive mini-brain that creates resistance in all of us.

I once helped facilitate a two-day annual retreat for Executive Forums, and it turned out amazingly because we were helping business-owners and leaders in the community understand their current business models and how to think in innovative ways. I've run meetings and given talks, but this experience pushed me outside my comfort zone—I had to fight "resistance" while preparing for the retreat, because growth is rarely comfortable.

Our lizard brain creates resistance within us—it's real too. It is the two-almond-shaped amygdala located deep in our brains. When we're afraid, mad, hungry, aroused, or experiencing some other strong emotion, it takes over.

It's kept our species alive for a long time, but it's not without its risks. It prevents you from overcoming natural fears by either running away or fighting—it creates the "flight or fight" response. Resistance is a combination of fear, doubt, anxiety, and rationalization generated by our lizard brain in order to protect us. You must overcome this in order to succeed—fight back against the negative self-talk, and control your own future.

Chapter 2

Focus and Execution

Focus and execution are two essential elements in any life plan. Without the ability to focus on what really matters, you lack the ability to plan. Without the ability to execute, you cannot put that plan into action. In this chapter we'll cover a range of related material, helping you build the focus and execution capabilities necessary.

Shiny Objects

I've been a "shiny object" guy for as long as I can remember. I've tried a number of organizational tools over the years. I started with checklists and progressed to the Day Timer program, Excel, Outlook Tasks, Outlook Folders, custom applications, Microsoft OneNote, mobile apps for my iPhone, and a number of others. None of these was a magic cure.

I began my career early. I co-founded and served as CEO for eighteen years at Pinnacle of Indiana—a large Microsoft-focused tech firm. One of my strengths is that I'm a futurist, which means I always look for the newest technologies and I'm constantly determining how to use technology and how to help our clients capitalize on it for success.

Unfortunately, this leads me to problems with focus. A friend recommended Dave Allen's *Getting Things Done* and watching TheSecretWeapon.org videos. I purchased the audiobook and hopped on the elliptical. It was incredible. I've been using the system for a couple of years at this point, and it's actually worked.

Continually striving for life-balance is very important to me. I think of the urgent and important grid of task management when I plan my week. Eighty percent of my week is in the business because there's no other option. The remaining twenty percent is working on the business, improving it because we choose to. This could be anything from process optimization to reporting to business intelligence, but at the end of the day that twenty percent is what moves us forward, and it requires focus in order to execute.

My planning and focus system isn't perfect, but I'm moving forward. It's let me enjoy life more, and my mind doesn't feel so crammed full. Read Dave Allen's book *Getting Things Done*, and give the videos on TheSecretWeapon.org a shot. You should also install Evernote on your devices. Simplify your life and give yourself the ability to focus and execute.

Revenue-Cost-Risk: What's Your Focus

A huge consideration in the ability to focus and execute is determining just what your focus is in the first place. What do you think about? Revenue? Cost? Risk? It's an important question and different people have different focuses. CEOs generally focus on revenue and growth, while wanting to manage risk. CFOs focus on cost and want risk managed. CIOs focus on risk management and support, while owners focus on all of these things.

Why do I use the term *risk management*? It's because *risk control* doesn't actually exist. Risk is always out there, and as soon as we think things are buttoned up tight a vulnerability comes along. I'm not preaching that you should live in fear. The key here is managing your exposure to risk. This applies across all systems.

I mention this because after we conduct technology whiteboard sessions of what typical companies have, we end up with a lot of systems and data everywhere. You have tons of manually created reports and spreadsheets with very few processes documented or integrated.

The solution is centralization and integration. Of course, you can't centralize everything, but you definitely don't need all those systems purchased on a whim to take care of a one-time pain point, usually with little or no consideration of the long-term effect on the company and costs associated with maintaining them.

CRM has come up in almost every session I've had, usually brought up by the CEO or owner. Let's talk about cost and risk for a second. How much is labor costing you on double-entering data and compiling reports? How much more time is spent determining what's going on with particular clients from opportunity, historical sales, or service standpoints?

You can research CRM systems (Microsoft CRM or Salesforce, for instance), but the key is to start pulling your systems together. It's the only way to have true relationships with customers. CRM stands for customer relationship management, and the right one can improve the revenue, cost, and risk components in your business.

- **Revenue** comes from better customer- and opportunity-management with real time metrics, alerts, etc.
- **Costs** come from data maintenance and removal of manually maintaining data in multiple areas and real-time reporting.
- **Risk**—All the data regarding a client, including emails correspondence between your company teams and the client, can automatically be captured in one spot. Now it is officially an asset.

If You Were Me ...

We all need new ways of developing focus, of seeing what's right in front of us. One of the best that I've found is asking people, "If you were me, what would you do?" The answers to that question gave me a lot of invaluable feedback and input, good ideas, and some much-needed perspective both on myself and where others were.

With all the transition issues associated with selling Pinnacle, merging two companies together, and rebuilding a group, I put that question away for a little while, but I recently dusted it off once more because it's just too valuable not to use. Seeking to understand and then to be understood is one of Steven Covey's golden rules, and it is simply a good thing to practice. However, a few factors can cause this question to misfire.

- Insecurity: If you are simply insecure, you won't get or hear feedback.
- Identity: If you don't know who you are and what you stand for, this won't work.
- Intimidation: If you're intimidating, it will be difficult for other people to open up or answer honestly.
- Indifference: This is the big one. If you don't care enough because you're afraid you might find an answer that will force you to rework a solution you've put your heart into, it simply won't work.

I struggled with this last one because you need to be humble and admit that your project or idea wasn't as good as you thought it was. That's hard to do sometimes. Getting perspective is particularly important when you're trying to communicate vision and provide good leadership. This applies at both work and home, which is something I overlooked.

I learned to apply this principle during daddy-daughter dates once per month. We'd sit down, whether to breakfast with donuts or lunch with chicken wings, and I'd discover nuggets of information that gave me better perspective on my daughters and how my wife and I could help.

Asking this question at home and at work is a good rhythm to get into because it makes you more aware, increases your emotional intelligence factor, and shows humility on your part—something sadly lacking in many people today. It builds trust and understanding, and having a few good people to cover your blinds spots while building a better understanding of yourself is important.

Projects and Priorities: Decision Making

How do you decide on your projects and priorities? Seth Godin's thoughts on the matter really sparked some interest in me. Do you know how you decide what you're going to do for the next hour, day, week, month, or year?

What are your metrics? Do you decide by any of these?

Easiest	Cheapest	Most Proven	Most Certain
Biggest Payoff	Most Fun	Most Convenient	Most Known
Most Unknown	Most Important	Most Urgent	Most Challenging

I've been challenging myself to think consciously about what I'm doing and what I'm working on, the important or urgent tasks. Covey talks about this in his book *4 Disciplines of Execution*, and I highly recommend reading it. Below, you'll find the quadrants he suggests for your tasks so you can distinguish the important tasks from the urgent ones.

	URGENT	NOT URGENT
IMPORTANT	**Quadrant 1** **important** **and urgent** *crises, deadlines, problems*	**Quadrant 2** **important** **but not urgent** *Relationships, planning, recreation*
NOT IMPORTANT	**Quadrant 4** **not important** **but urgent** *interruptions, meetings, activities*	**Quadrant 3** **not important** **not urgent** *Time wasters, pleasant activities, trivia*

As my company's CSO my overall goal is to ensure we're adding value to our customers. I do this by researching technologies and the ever-changing solutions out there. My day-to-day tasks involve meeting with clients, responding to emails, managing a division of amazing folks—all of this is working *in* the business.

My critical activities and important goals are tasks that work *on* moving the business forward, including process improvements, new systems, and new partnerships. Distractions and interruptions occur of course. There's no perfect answer to structuring your time, but knowing which way you want to go and where your feet are pointed is an excellent starting point.

Setting Realistic Targets

The goals we set for ourselves are integral parts of focus and execution. Tons of books, blogs, and websites are dedicated to helping you hit your goals if you know what they are. Part of intentional living is planning, being organized, and thinking about the important things, including realistic targets and goals.

When my Aunt Rene passed away, the kids, cousins, and extended family pulled together to have a gathering to honor her and to help the family through this time of grief. It was an amazing celebration of someone's life. It also gave me insight into my own goals and targets.

I ended up having my butt kicked by my Uncle John in ping-pong. It all started with my cousin Bob and I drinking a beer and playing ping-pong with the younger nieces and nephews. It was fun, and then Bob and I started playing pretty competitively. We played a few sets, and I held my own even though he beat me in each set. So when Uncle John came in, I had my ego nicely in check.

I asked if he'd like to play, and we gave it a go. He won all three games. When Bob played him, it was with the same results. Then he trounced me a second time even though I gave it my all. When it was over, I asked just how old he was. He calmly replied that he was seventy. I processed that, and really started wondering just how I could have been beaten by a seventy-year-old. That's negative self-talk, but it happened.

I came out of that experience with a new target—I thought to be that agile, quick, calm, and intentional would be an amazing thing. His humility in giving all the credit to playing with his grandkids also spurred another target—humble agility.

Target adjustment: look for lessons in life to ensure you're setting realistic targets that help you live intentionally and become a better person.

Winning vs. Earning

There's a huge focus in our society on winning, usually at all costs. Do you remember the meme back in the 1990s: "He who dies with the most toys wins"? That's very telling. Winning seems to be what it's all about, but is it really?

Every year my wife and I celebrate her cousin's birthday at the blue chip casino with her and her husband. We don't really go for the gaming—we love the restaurant. We're not big gamblers, but we do have fun within a specific set limit for the games.

The last time we went, it was a little different. I'd just started listening to *Business Secrets from the Bible* by Rabbi Daniel Lapin. Secret 13 talks about the difference between winning a sum of money and earning a sum of money. He goes into detail on a number of subjects, but several important points jumped out at me. My experience in the casino only served to reinforce them. Here are some of the most pertinent to living an intentional life:

- There is no phrase in the Hebrew language for "winning money," only for "earning money."
- He uses an example of going to a casino: "I went to the casino and won money, by which you mean you gained money that someone else lost."
- Earning money is clearly superior to winning money, because when you earn money, two parties benefit: the one who earns the money and the one who makes a purchase or receives a service.

The scenario where two parties win is the only way. Building relationships, doing the right thing, and earning a fair living should be in all of our life-plans. I'm not saying that I won't go to the casino—there's a good deal of entertainment there, but I certainly won't go thinking that I'm going to win big, or that it will change my life. Ensuring your purpose is clear will allow you to live a healthy, more fulfilled life with focus and the ability to execute.

What's Most Important?

Understanding the need for focus and execution is all well and good, but it's useless if you can't decide what's most important right now. Life and work can be overwhelming with all the complexities and the immediately-connected world in which we live. You have to be able to decide what's important right now.

History is done and gone. Tomorrow hasn't yet been written. It's what we do right now that moves us in the direction we want to go. When we say yes to one thing we say no to something else, or at a minimum we're saying we're moving on to other items on the priority list. It's essential to know your priorities because it makes it easier to say no to requests or options when they come up.

My priorities are as follows:

- God
- Me
- My wife
- My children
- Extended family
- Friends
- My career
- Finances

- Ministry

When someone asks me to go out for a quick drink but I had a date planned with my wife, it's easy to say no. My wife is third on the list, which is above friends, so there's no conflict. I recently had to do this with a vacation. When my eldest and second eldest daughters turned twenty-one and twenty respectively, the pressures of going back to school, getting ready for college, work, and more convinced my wife and I to head down to Nashville to celebrate with them. It was an easy "yes" because it was a simple matter of determining priority.

What are your priorities? Are you saying yes to things that you should be declining?

Chapter 3

You're More Than Your Job

Who are you, at heart? I don't mean what you do. I don't mean your position at work. You're more than your job, and until you stop defining yourself solely by your role in the workplace you won't be able to live intentionally. You're more than your job, and this chapter will help you realize just how much more.

Are You Your Job?

When someone asks you about yourself, do you start with your role at work, or you as a person? I love asking this question. Normally, the first thought is their role at work. As we spend eight to ten hours per day at work, that should probably be expected.

However you need to know your true identity. I figured that out a few years back and I continue to work on it. While

I cofounded Pinnacle at the age of twenty-eight, I came to the conclusion twelve years later that I had to separate my role from my ownership. Let me clarify: just because I co-owned the business didn't mean I deserved the role of CEO. Owners get this wrong all too often. They feel they deserve that role and need it to ensure control. It often stems from the entrepreneurial and narcissistic traits in owners.

In Good to Great, Jim Collins tells us you have to get the right people on the bus, then get the right people in the right seats on the bus. It takes a deal of soul searching and being honest with yourself to determine if you're in the right seat. If you're not sure, ask yourself the following questions:

- Where am I the most productive?
- What do I enjoy the most?
- What can only I do?
- What am I the best at that will contribute to the most?
- Am I maximizing my own value?

Do You Allow Failure?

Let me be blunt. Real leaders allow failure. It's tough, and not allowing failure is a common mistake. No one likes to fail, and no one wants to watch someone else fail. However, that's how you build people up. Training yourself to respond versus react to mistakes is extremely important for growth. Our team adopted a "retrospective" process to review when mistakes are discovered. It leads to improvement and alleviation—or at least minimization—of mistakes. It goes something like this:

- First we map out what happened using a flow chart, timeline, or another useful tool.

- Next we discuss what worked.
- We discuss what didn't work or completely failed.
- We determine what could be improved.
- We determine how to incorporate these improvements into the process for future cases.

To make this work, you must be a Model 2 leader, as Model 1 leaders generally don't allow this type of interaction. Where do you fall in terms of leadership type?

Model 1 Traits:

- Defensive, inconsistent, controlling, fearful of being vulnerable
- Limited or doesn't allow freedom of choice or risk taking
- Controls the environment, defines and controls tasks
- Time-based versus performance- or scoreboard-based

Model 2 Traits:

- Facilitator, promotes collaboration, choice, and free thinking to accomplish tasks
- Target-based thinking vs. task-based thinking
- Allows and encourages freedom of thought and idea testing
- Tasks are jointly controlled
- Learning-oriented environment

Obviously, the second style leads to increased long-term effectiveness, while the first one does not. The most important thing is to have good hiring practices in place so you get the right people on the bus. You also need to let people "fail forward" in order to grow both as employees or staff and as individuals.

Is It the Destination or the Journey?

Life is a journey—that is more than just a truism. It's what I believe, and what I base my actions and decisions on. It's not the destination that matters, and in order to live an intentional life you must understand that it's what happens between milestones that matters most.

When we used to go on vacations my family and I would have the destination as the beginning of the vacation. We changed that a few years back, and now when we pull out of the garage, we say a quick prayer and state that the vacation has begun. We start enjoying it. The journey is part of the vacation, which changes our mindset. Everything that happens on the journey is an experience we can enjoy.

It wasn't always this way. We used to be in a rush to get to where we were going so we could relax and really start the vacation. That led to frustration and annoyance, conflict, and stress. It made the trip seem three times longer than it really was.

The concept of enjoying the journey applies not just to your personal life, but to your professional life as well. At work, you should have a business plan with objectives, timelines, and a technology roadmap that are all aligned. This is the key to consciously making the plan, executing the plan, and enjoying the journey of doing the tasks to accomplish your goals.

You'll always have crap to deal with in life. I call this the "crap factor" and tell people that we all have about twenty percent crap during our week that we must be ready to handle. Get your plan together, expect to handle some crap, and enjoy the journey.

Who Are You Going to Be?

We're all presented with turning points in our lives, often many of them. A few years back I was asked to help with baptisms during a period when I was pulling together my life-plan. I had talked about aligning technology with business strategy for a long time, but I never really dialed it in until my life-plan consciously focused me on how I wanted to be remembered: not for how much money I had or tasks I'd accomplished, but who I was and how I helped others.

Knowing who you are and what you stand for is probably the biggest turning point you can make in your life. Too often we work hard at trying to be a good spouse, parent, friend, or employee, but if we don't know our priorities how can we be successful at this?

Life is short. Make the most of it. My mom passed away when I was a freshman in high school, and my dad passed away in early 2014. Understand your past and what made you who you are, so you can capitalize on that today. It leads to a happier you, a happier family, and a good life at work and home.

In the same vein, it's important to align and prioritize both your work and personal life. I've been doing this for a long time, but when I aligned my priorities, all aspects of my life became more fulfilling and fun. Align yourself with your life strategy. Know who you are and what you stand for. Know what you want to be remembered for, and create your plan.

Getting in Rhythm with Your Team and Your Family

The right rhythm is important for more things than just music. It's vital for your personal and business life as well. I have regular date nights with my wife and daughters. Those are an essential element of staying in rhythm with them so I learn things and can address issues in a timely manner before they boil over. This rhythm, called meeting rhythm, is commonly used in business but also applies at home, with friends, and with family.

I hold a daily huddle meeting at 8:08 AM with the direct reports of my division, That meeting is significant for its ability to keep us in synch. Our huddle helps alleviate a lot of the distracting noise that keeps us from being productive and healthy. Rhythm creates a healthy culture, which acts as a company multiplier.

Think about it: when you are healthy, you do everything better. You think more clearly and deeply. You are more productive. You're happier. You treat others better. A healthy person and a healthy culture truly do multiply outcomes. Of course you need the right type and number of meetings to foster a healthy culture, but there are only a few you can use.

- **Annual Meeting:** This type of meeting is for discussing progress on last year's goals, and to set and get alignment among your management team on goals you plan for the next year.
- **Quarterly Meeting:** You measure progress toward your year-end goals and discuss what's needed in the next thirteen weeks to meet the plan.
- **Monthly Meeting:** These meetings focus on monthly learning. They are opportunities for the management team to start developing the next levels in the organization. It should be two to four

hours, and the extended management team should review progress and financial results and make any necessary decisions.

- **Weekly Meetings:** These should be strategic meetings, focusing on specific issues. Discuss progress toward your top critical initiatives while also looking at key performance indicators (KPIs), customer feedback, and employee feedback. Don't cover everything every week. This forces weekly meetings to be shallow and to run for too long. Pick a focus each month or quarter.
- **Daily Huddles:** These should last no more than fifteen minutes, and should be a combination pep talk and focus meeting. Everyone should be involved in a daily huddle, but not everyone in the same huddle. Break things up across the business. Talk about where people are stuck, focus on the right activities, and build better efficiency.
- **Purpose-Specific Meetings:** These are on-the-fly meetings that should only include those directly involved and should be centered on a specific issue, problem, or purpose.

When done correctly, the right meeting rhythm will help you and your team get in synch and stay there, while saving you a significant amount of time and many headaches.

CFOs and Prom Dresses

Do you have any idea how many types of prom dresses there are? As the father of three daughters, I had a crash course, especially with my youngest and her friend. As I stared at the dizzying array of options in a sea of dresses with other daughters and their parents all in search of the perfect dress, I started thinking about the different types of CFOs. It's an odd correlation, but can you really blame me?

It's important that you determine the type of CFO on your team. Knowing the CFO type is an essential factor in ensuring you get the truth on best practices, accurate numbers, and to establish a relationship of trust. When looking at your CFO, you should know how they're naturally wired, as well as how to cover their weaknesses to ensure your business strategy is aligned financially and technically. Here's the lowdown on CFO classifications:

1. **The Numbers CFO**
   This person has experience in multiple finance positions including auditing, financial planning, and controller. They're usually an internal hire and have a strong understanding of company operations.
2. **The Strategist CFO**
   This professional is usually hired outside of finance, and has experience in operations, marketing, and general management. He or she runs a tight ship and has major influence with teams and in business decisions.
3. **The KPI CFO**
   These CFOs love their scoreboards, and measurable targets are their focus. Goals are clearly communicated, and they ensure best practices with metrics, costs, and standards without bias driving them.
4. **The Growth CFO**
   This is the least common type of CFO, as the role is typically one for the CEO or COO. Growth is their target and key motivation, and they're usually experienced in mergers and acquisitions, private equity, or venture capitalism.

All four CFO classifications contain great strengths, and most can have multiple traits that fall into different categories. The same can be said for CEOs who don't have a CFO on their team. If you don't have a CFO, your responsibilities as the CEO will include paying attention to bookkeeping and financial management, creating and using KPIs to align business strategies, and keeping a strong eye on leveraging technologies.

It's essential that you are concerned with the financial and technological direction of your company, and that you definitely know what type of CFO you have. The key is to determine which type fits you and ensures productive business synergy, just like the night at the prom.

CEO Action Plan

Determine what type of CFO you have on your team, and then their weaknesses to ensure they're covered. You may have to play this role personally. Keep IT accountability on the table, as you must ensure it's a strategic asset not just a cost center. Have your CFO take the Strengths Finder 2.0 test to give you both some insight.

Business strategy is about people, strategy, execution, and cash. Make sure you have the right CFO, as they're usually watching the cash.

Keeping the Humble/Hungry Balance

I've found that two words are key to a life and career of continuous improvement and growth. Whether you're just starting out or you've achieved the pinnacle of success, it's important to remember to be both humble and hungry with the right balance.

Be Humble

- Never believe you know it all. Be a lifelong learner, always seeking to grow and improve.
- See everyone as a teacher, no matter how different their walk of life might be. They all have lessons to teach.
- Be open to new ideas and strategies in all areas of your life.
- Don't let your ego rule you, but don't let criticism sink you either.
- Be kind to everyone, and let people know they matter.
- Live with humility, because the minute you think you've arrived at the door of greatness it will slam in your face.
- Humility doesn't mean you think less of yourself. It means you think of yourself less.

Be Hungry

- Follow your passion and improve continuously—dream.
- Seek out new ideas, new strategies, and new ways to push yourself out of that comfort zone.
- Invest time, energy, and dedication to be your best, and let God do the rest.
- Become the hardest worker you know.
- Be willing to pay the price greatness demands. Don't be average.
- Love the process, and you'll love what it produces.
- Leave a legacy.
- Focus on where you are and where you're going, not on where you've been.
- Quest for excellence in all areas of your life.

Stay humble and hungry, and everything will fall into place.

Chapter 4

Technology: Are You Stymieing Progress?

Technology is everywhere today. It enables better productivity, delivers capabilities impossible just a few years ago, and aids businesses in every way imaginable. It can also be daunting—even worrisome if you're not familiar with it. Are you stymieing technology and progress in your company?

Are You the Bottleneck?

Are you the bottleneck for technology in your business? I've seen it happen too many times over the years, and it has a major impact on the culture of a company, the engagement of teams and employees, and even on the bottom line.

Common Technology Mistakes

To help you determine if you're bottlenecking technology in your business, let's go over a few of the more common tech-related mistakes.

The owner is in a role because he started the business versus being in the role where his strengths lie.

Obviously, the business owner must have some intelligence, but over time, that can create a false sense of success. Owners start believing they can do everything, especially when it comes to technology.

The answer to this issue is simple. Just let go. Put some metrics in place so you can measure at a high level. You know what these should be for your business. Just step out of the way and let the right person implement technology.

The owner/CEO is getting filtered and very opinionated information from the person in charge of IT regarding the technology direction.

Being in charge of IT can be daunting—these professionals are expected to know everything from security to databases and applications. That just can't happen. I break down IT into three groups to help explain the technology side of a business. This usually helps the owner/CEO get their head around it.

The three groups are the "Break/Fix Support Role," the "Server/Network Role" and the "Chief Information Officers (CIO) Role."

The first role is generally filled by technicians who handle things like computer problems, basic network issues, and the like.

The second role is filled by engineers—those who handle server issues, connectivity items, and security.

The final role is one of strategy, and dictates the direction technology goes within the business. The CIO should work hand in hand with the CEO and CFO to align business strategy with the technology strategy. Depending on the size of the business, these roles might be filled by several people, a few people, or even just one person (in the case of a small business).

The role of the CIO is generally the most problematic, as they have the knowledge necessary to give the CEO the information needed, but this information can be very biased and even flawed. The real issue here is that the CIO often incorporates two other roles that should be separate—the "applications" role and the "data" role. Both of these roles have significant influence over accounting, customer information systems, desktop applications, line of business systems, specialty applications, and how they come together.

If your business has all these roles covered, then you're in the clear. In fact you're the exception to the rule. If you don't, then there's some work that needs to be done in identifying role-holders and determining responsibilities.

Weights and Data Don't Lie

My brother and I got our first set of weights from a garage sale back when I was in third grade. He's only fourteen months younger than I am, so it worked out that we could both start pumping iron together. It was a little early for both of us, but we lived in the inner city on the west side of South Bend, so it helped us avoid getting beat up regularly.

I learned early on that our weights never lied. Either you could lift them or you couldn't. To be able to lift heavier weights, you had to put in the time and effort. You had to push yourself outside your comfort zone. The weights never changed though. I did. I often think about the truth of weights and data when I work with businesses to formulate roadmaps. I'm a "data freak," and I push hard here all the time. I pose questions like: Where is the data? Who's updating it? Who's validating its accuracy? How many versions are there? Are you re-keying it multiple times?

Inevitably there are multiple versions of the truth, meaning similar but inaccurate data. The result is duplicate tracking at a minimum. The number of Excel sheets being kept and the presence of financials in Excel is usually the big tip off for me. This is bad for a number of reasons.

First, there's the effort required to update your spreadsheets rather than just gatekeeping and validation. Centralization and integration are key components, particularly with all the tools available today that let you analyze data with little effort. For CFOs, getting the team out of duplicate entry as much as possible is vital. Getting the team back into controls and analytics should be a target as businesses can make timelier, more accurate decisions with the correct information presented the right way.

There's no reason not to have real-time data, reports, and business insight at your fingertips today. Microsoft and many others offer free tools that integrate with Excel and other systems.

It's time to get out of manual business mode. Automation of bad data only delivers bad results faster. Centralize, integrate, and maintain data accuracy.

Embrace Generations for IT Adoption Success

Once upon a time generations in the workforce were classified by age rather than their ability to adapt to new technologies. That's no longer the case. There's also the notion that older generations are less willing to adapt to new technology, but that's not really true either. In fact Baby

Boomers and "Matures" (those born pre-1946) are among the fastest adopters of tablet computers and other new technology.

I used to believe there should be separate processes for the different generations, but I was proven wrong. Rather, technology adoption is about getting the right people in the right seats doing the right things—sound familiar?.

I now regularly challenge myself to consider people's strengths, attitudes, and leadership that allows for training and change. Attitude and willingness to learn new things are both paramount, but leadership is also vital. If it's not there, the client and I have a long discussion as I don't want to work on a project that's destined to fail right out of the gate.

With the right leader, a company can thrive with all generations working together, maximizing their potential. Don't be afraid to change roles and invest in people. Gen Y got a reputation for being the "deserving" and mobile-only generation, but with training and mentoring all generations can help each other.

BYOD: Why It's Actually a Good Thing

There's some natural resistance to the bring-your-own-device (BYOD) movement. Superficially it makes sense, but it's actually the wrong stance. BYOD is a good thing. In fact a study by Gartner shows that thirty-eight percent of organizations will stop providing devices to workers by 2016. The study predicts by 2017 fifty percent of employees will bring their own devices to work.

Embracing the BYOD movement offers a number of benefits including reduced costs, better agility, and increased productivity. However, there are some considerations here. Serious consequences of embracing BYOD without strong support and decisions from the CEO and CFO can lead to security issues, costly software incompatibilities, and financial ramifications. CEOs and CFOs must work hand in hand with CIOs to stay engaged in setting strategy, policies, and usage standards.

Still, the benefits outweigh the risks, even with subsidies provided to compensate team members for the use of their personal devices. The upside is huge. Don't fight it or you'll end up losing the opportunity to motivate your team. Don't get stuck in the past. Technology and BYOD are transforming the way we work and communicate.

Trapped in IT Jail

Do you feel trapped by IT? I recently spoke at a CFO summit about emerging technologies, trends, managing IT, the cloud, and a few other topics. One of the points was the reporting structure of the CIO or IT manager. The CIO reporting structure has shifted to reporting to the CFO. This is good for many reasons, but it means the CFO must now try to understand technology and its impact on the business.

Some CFOs glaze over during executive team meetings because they don't fully comprehend the technology. They're fully engaged through the accounting, ERP, and business process discussions, but when we hit the technology, database, and integration layers, the mental checkout begins. That's dangerous. Some CIOs aren't following best practices because they aren't retooling their skills to coincide with the rapid pace of technological change.

The bottom line is this: CEOs, owners and CFOs need to think of technology like they do audits. Having an outside firm come in and audit IT should be a common practice, just like auditing your books. You can't know everything, and having someone outside take a look at your IT setup, identify risks, and make recommendations is vital. You'll at least know where you stand.

IT: Cost Center or Strategic Asset?

IT should be more than just a cost center. It should be a strategic asset essential for business growth, stability, and success. I've spoken on this topic for a long time. However many executives—while appreciating the strategic value of IT—nevertheless feel that their current IT teams aren't cutting it, and things need to change.

With the cloud evolution IT resources will shift, and a retooling of attitude will need to take place. Proper IT representation must be present at business strategy team meetings, including all layers of IT from infrastructure to application and integration.

Current IT budgets and spending on infrastructure are starting to decrease as the transition to the cloud takes place. Retooling your IT resources is critical to capitalize on IT in your business. Those resources are now finite, which is a problem for businesses hoping to capitalize on IT as a business accelerator. Every study I've read has shown that attracting and retaining top IT talent will be a significant challenge in the immediate future. To do this you'll need to improve your culture, energy, and morale in the IT department. Offer more competitive salaries and better benefits. Provide clearer, more structured career paths. You must offer more cutting-edge, exciting work within IT.

It's a lot to take in, but ensuring that you have a well-trained IT team that understands and is aligned with corporate objectives is essential to your success.

The Cloud: Getting Onboard

The cloud: it's one of those terms that everyone knows, but very few actually understand. What is it? Where is it? How does it work? What does it do? The cloud is the ultimate IT resource management tool. It allows you to manage IT assets effectively while simultaneously decreasing the time and costs required to manage them. That allows you to focus on your core business.

One of the most important advantages of the cloud is its elasticity. You can turn up your usage demands and then lower them during down periods. This includes computing power, electricity usage, and everything else. You only pay for what you use. It delivers a number of other advantages, including speed, agility, flexibility, innovation, and economic benefits.

Of course, it's not without its challenges. Governance, cloud environments, security, and privacy are all concerns here. Here are my recommendations for your business where the cloud is concerned.

Cloud Backup: This should be a no-brainer. Tape drivers are dead. Cloud backup systems are plentiful, cheap, and reliable. In many instances, they also work as disaster recovery solutions too.

Email: Your email should be in the cloud, without a doubt. Ninety-five percent of emails are spam or malware, and by putting email in the cloud, you open up more computing power. You offload the need to secure and patch the system; upgrades are done by someone else, and it's cheaper.

CRM Systems: Cloud applications can handle your CRM or centralized contact management system more easily than you can do it in house. They're also faster and cheaper.

Financial and ERP: This is a mixed bag. Manufacturers should keep things in house, but financial and distribution operations can move to the cloud without too much worry.

Document Management: Get this out of your business. There's simply no reason to keep your documents local with the wide range of solutions out there today, whether you use Office 365, SharePoint, or something else.

Document Imaging and Management: Space in the cloud is cheap, so move this out of your business.

Cloud computing allows you to focus on your core business instead of worrying about IT issues. Don't be afraid to partner with an outside firm on this, as they have expertise and resources that are hard to find internally.

C-Suite: Knowing Your Strengths

Business is comprised of three separate components: people, process, and systems. Do you know where you fit into the box below? If you don't, it would be wise to determine just where you do, and then know your strengths.

CEO	CFO	CIO/IT Manager
Knows Technology	The Numbers	Strategy/Leader
Aware	Strategist	Business Optimization
Faking It	KPI	Operational/Tactical
Total Delegation	Growth	Technical

CEO (Chief Executive Officer)

- **Knows Technology**: You understand technology as a whole and can help drive metrics, processes, and capitalize on technology as a strategic asset. You are on board with aligning the business strategy with technology.

- **Aware**: You know enough to keep up in business meetings, and keep learning and asking the right questions. However you want to stay focused on the business strategy.
- **Faking It**: You stay focused on business strategy and say little during technology discussions. You insist on bringing the discussion back to the point of whether it will help the company meet its goals, which is something you definitely understand. You're careful of speaking when technology is an integral part of the solution.
- **Total Delegation**: You defer all decisions to your CIO or CFO, while doing vision and strategy from the total business viewpoint with very little in the way of technology discussion.

CFO (Chief Financial Officer)

- **The Numbers**: You have experience in multiple positions: finance, auditing, financial planning, controller, and so on. You're usually an internal hire, moving up the ladder.
- **Strategist**: You're usually an outside hire, with experience in marketing, general management, and operations. You run a tight ship and have business influence.
- **KPI**: You love measurable targets, clear goals, and scoreboards. You follow best practices without bias.
- **Growth**: You're the least common of CFOs. Growth is your target, and you probably have experience in

private equity, venture capitalism, or mergers and acquisitions.

CIO (Chief Information Officer)

- **Strategist/Leader**: You take a structured approach to moving IT forward and building its reputation for delivering business results. You liaise closely with other C-level executives to ensure business alignment. You might also exhibit various other traits, but you do so within a defined, well-organized framework.
- **Business Optimization**: You can be a charismatic leader and often parachute into a situation for a short period to take control, optimize, and then hand it off so you can move on to the next thing. You take a detailed, project-by-project view. You work with C-level executives for incremental and quantum improvements to drive the business forward but have a tendency to ignore smaller issues.
- **Operational/Tactical**: You keep IT on an even keel, and will solve the immediate issues and upgrade legacy technology when necessary. You're likely to drive incremental change and evolution but unlikely to "set the world on fire."
- **Technical**: You're happiest when talking technology. You probably moved up through the ranks. You're more likely to discuss solutions than strategy, and you love having the latest gadget. You may have a tendency to have lots of IT-driven projects that aren't championed by the business, and you run the risk of having technology for technology's sake.

It's essential that you are aware of your team. This awareness will change the reporting structure in your business, especially when it comes to IT. Depending on the type of CFO you have, the CEO and CFO may actually jointly manage the CIO position. I've seen a lot of technology implementations go south because decision-makers failed to understand the type of C-Suite in place.

Understanding your C-Suite type has a great deal to do with capitalizing on technology as a strategic asset. Get outside help to assess your team if necessary. Some of this can be learned and some of this is just knowing your strengths in order to capitalize on them.

Know where you fit in, and know your strengths. Take the Strengths Finders assessment, and cover your weaknesses. Hire someone to cover them if necessary. Outsource a portion of those weaknesses to make sure they're covered. Doing so will save you more than you think. Have fun with knowing your weaknesses, and don't be insecure. It helps no one.

Chapter 5

The Lie of Multitasking and the Enemy of Progress

Multitasking: we all try to do it, and if we're honest with ourselves we all fail at it. Multitasking is just one enemy of progress. There are myriad other threats out there that derail your productivity and actually lead to a lack of progress while masquerading as enhancements. In this chapter we'll dig into the lie of multitasking and the enemies of progress.

Multitasking – Get Thirty Percent of Your Day Back

The multitasking mantra has become so ingrained in our culture that it's become accepted as the truth. Sadly it's not. You can't multitask. Neither can your team. Sure, you can switch back and forth between tasks quickly, but that's not multitasking. Only computers are capable of true multitasking and multiprocessing. I've had to address this lie and its effects within businesses too many times.

The reality here is that you can only focus on one task at a time, no matter how fast you switch back and forth. Sadly, doing so reduces your productivity by a significant amount. In fact, you can lose up to thirty percent of your day—and your team is losing the same amount. You know how long it takes to get back in the groove to finish a task if you have a lot of stops and starts.

The key here is to block out uninterrupted time for bigger tasks and to get two monitors on everyone's desk. It's that simple.

Every desktop or laptop should have two monitors. That will give you back thirty percent of your day. It removes the need to switch back and forth when checking schedules, editing documents, writing documents, conducting research, updating spreadsheets, and pretty much everything else. Most CFOs look at the cost of adding dual monitors and don't look at the corresponding thirty percent increase in productivity for every person, every single workday. You're essentially gaining *seventy-six days* back annually for each person on the team. Think about that for just a second.

The same thing applies to multi-focusing. You can only focus on *one* thing at a time. By focusing on one thing as often as you can you increase your productivity, your quality, and even reduce your stress levels.

Driving into Storms

"Driving into storms" simply means diving straight into issues you face. Do you drive into them, or do you try to go around? I recently learned that Colorado is one of the few states that has both buffalo and cows in it. How does this relate? Well, it turns out that when a storm is coming from the west over the Rockies, the cows start to run from it. The storm usually catches them, and they stay in it for a long time because they're running with it. Buffalo, on the other hand, wait for the storm to hit the mountains, and then run right into it and out the other side. They minimize their time in the storm by charging straight through its heart.

Simply put: It's better to get it over and done with than to sit on it and prolong the misery and problems. If you try to avoid it or drive around the storm, it usually gets worse and ruins the other things that you want to get done, sometimes for a long time. It also builds up anxiety, which can make you not enjoy your day or cause people around you not to enjoy being near you. I use the same principle in the retrospectives we do with our team, which we discussed earlier in this book.

You know when you need to address something, because you feel it in your gut. Trust your gut on most things and if you're not sure, talk to the person covering your blind spots. Remember—drive into storms, minimize the fallout, and emerge stronger and better on the other side.

Control Your Day or It Will Control You

Are you controlling your day, or does it control you? It's an interesting concept to ponder, as many of us get behind in the beginning and then spend the rest of the day playing catch up. For many, days like this string together into weeks or even months until we feel it's impossible to get ahead. Our lives are out of balance and we feel out of control. It's not a good place to be.

In today's tech-driven world, it's easy to get caught up and even lost in the 24/7 interconnectedness. It's easy to blow valuable time surfing the web or on Facebook and Twitter with absolutely nothing to show for it. Technology can be a help or a hindrance depending on how you master it. It should be a tool that brings value and contributes to personal and professional goals and dreams.

I believe in continuous improvement. It's essential for an intentional life. As such, I constantly look for ways to improve my processes and adjust my routines so I can accomplish my goals. I recently changed my morning routine. However it wasn't some spur of the moment thing or some ill-conceived and soon forgotten New Year's resolution. I spent seven months planning and studying before I made that change. I even hired a coach to help with my faith habits.

The immediate upshot of this was I realized that owning your day starts in the morning, but it's decided the night before. A long time ago, I read that you rarely win debates with yourself in the morning, so you must decide what you are going to do in advance. That means if you're going to get up and workout, you decide the night before. You put out your clothes, and when the alarm goes off you get up and do it.

Using Michael Hyatt's *Ideal Week Excel Template*, I created my ideal week. I determined what time to get up, what time to go to bed, when email needed to be processed, and when my most productive time is. It was truly eye-opening, and something I recommend everyone do as it sheds light on what you want to do versus what you are doing.

In the end, this simple change helped me in life-balance, work effectiveness, and my happiness meter is continuously going up.

The Enemy of Progress: Perfection

At the beginning of this chapter, I mentioned the "enemies" of progress. The pursuit of perfection is one of the most important to understand, primarily because we're taught that perfection is not only desirable but attainable. It's not.

The drive for perfection in business leads to what I call "analysis paralysis." You're so worried about doing everything right that your forward momentum comes to a screeching halt. Don't do that. Focus on making the best decisions you can at the time. This applies especially to technology because it evolves far too fast to have a perfect plan.

I tell my clients they should have a 90-day plan, a 1-year plan, a 3-year outlook, and a 10-year simple long-term vision. The 90-day and 1-year plan can be detailed and granular, but the farther out you look, the fuzzier things become.

Let me reiterate: you do need a real strategy. If it doesn't pass the two points below, you don't have a strategy.

1. What you're planning to do actually matters to your existing and potential customers.
2. It differentiates you from your competition.

#2 is a reminder about quality. The paradox here is that making the best quality decisions may not be perfect for the sake of progress. This happens frequently with services and products. Just look at Windows. It wasn't the best when it was first released, but they did capture the market.

One of my favorite quotes comes from George S. Patton: "A good plan, violently executed now, is better than a perfect plan next week." That really sums it all up. Make the best decision you can today, and be agile with change. Alignment of the team is the most important thing. When everyone knows the targets, changes and resets can motivate rather than deflate.

Why Wouldn't Cha

I love the phrase, "Why wouldn't cha?" My brother introduced me to it one year at a weekend camp. It was his way of saying, "Why not? Let's go for it." I started using the *why-wouldn't-cha* phrase after doing strategic planning sessions with clients. It sounds basic, but once you've gathered and analyzed the facts and the team has poked holes in the plan to make sure it's solid, the next statement is, "Why wouldn't cha do this?"

Over the years, this phrase has reminded me of the "Tyranny of the OR, or the Genius of the AND," from Jim Collins' perennial bestselling business book, *Good to Great*. Astute readers will notice that I've recommended this book before—it's well worth the read. I love the "genius of AND," and I apply in all areas of my life. Few things in life are actually either/or, one or the other but not both. There are always more options, more choices, and more possibilities than we think. We just need to look for the *and*. I ask myself, "Why does it have to be an *or* when in many cases it can be an *and*?"

As a business leader you have the option to:

- Build people *and* discipline them.
- Love them *and* pay them.
- Care about them *and* demand better from them.
- Be strong *and* insecure.
- Create a strong trust culture *and* fire people.

True leaders know how to grow others, build trust, and communicate vision. There is so much energy wasted in creating false or negative beliefs when team members do not understand leadership's vision. Just be a leader that leads *and* shares a vision even though things can and will change. You'll find your team rallies around the company when they know what you're thinking, where you're taking the company, and what you expect in terms of their contribution.

If you can create a strong team based on a shared vision, built on trust and solid communication, and one that looks for the *and* rather than the "Tyranny of the OR," my question to you is, "Why wouldn't cha?"

The Value of Emotional Intelligence

I mentioned emotional intelligence earlier in this book, and now's the time to dig into it. *Emotional Intelligence* by Daniel Goleman sits on my bookshelf, and I regularly reference it. Recently, I found the need to pull it out once more.

One of my daughters was struggling to regulate her responses, so I decided to quickly educate her on emotional intelligence. I thought it might be good for her to learn how to respond when she gets upset. It was an educational opportunity, so I shared my explanation of EI with her. As I explained to her, it can be broken down into five different classifications:

1. Self-Awareness: You recognize your own emotions and how they affect your thoughts and behavior. You know your strengths and weaknesses, and have self-confidence.
2. Self-Regulation: This is your ability to control impulsive feelings and behaviors, to manage your

emotions in healthy ways, to take initiative and follow through on commitments, while adapting to changes.

3. Social Skills and Awareness: You can understand the emotions, concerns and needs of others. You can pick up on emotional cues and feel comfortable socially, while recognizing the structure in groups and organizations.
4. Relationship Management/Motivation: You know how to develop and maintain good relationships, while communicating clearly and inspiring others. You work well in a team and can manage conflict.
5. Empathy: This is the ability to empathize with others, to put yourself in their shoes.

Individuals with high emotional intelligence can recognize their own emotional state, as well as that of others, and engage with people in ways that draw them out. You can use this understanding of emotions to relate better to other people, form healthier relationships, and achieve greater success in both your personal and professional lives.

How are you doing in these five areas? They're essential, because EI affects your performance at work, your physical health, your mental health, and your relationships. Being aware of how you rank in these areas can help provide better life-balance, productivity, and overall happiness. Improving your emotional intelligence requires that you develop key skills for controlling and managing overwhelming stress and becoming more effective in communication.

- Develop the ability to quickly reduce stress in a moment in virtually any setting.

- Recognize your emotions and keep them from overwhelming you.
- Develop the ability to connect with others emotionally, even nonverbally.
- Develop the ability to use humor and play to stay connected in challenging situations.
- Develop the ability to resolve conflicts confidently and in a positive way.

The key here is awareness and regulation. Once you're aware, which requires someone to help, you can start regulating your responses to become a better leader and a better person.

Humble Intelligence

Humility is an integral part of intentional living. Humble intelligence ties into that and expands on it in many different ways. Mastering this skill can help you become a much more effective leader, and even a better person.

I was once asked to step into a meeting between some very intelligent people. The meeting turned into a heated discussion with some ruffled feathers. After we'd resolved everything it continued to nag at me, and I realized that I needed to respond—as opposed to react, which is very different and should be avoided. I did a retrospective and realized that the root of the issue was a single individual. This person was definitely smart enough, but lacked some important interpersonal skills, which isn't that rare with highly intelligent people.

We sat down and discussed ways to change the situation. Some of the items we came up with include the following:

- Use "we" statements as opposed to "I."

- Use questions when you need something, rather than making demands.
- Listen more. Talk less.
- Don't jump in when someone else is asked a question.
- Ask clarifying questions.
- Use eye contact as much as possible.

Each of these items ties into operating in your strengths area, making you, your coworkers, and your family and friends happier. Work is people, process, and systems. Family is people, communication, and understanding our differences to balance each other out. Know your strengths and your emotional intelligence score, and be hyper aware of you, so you can self-regulate in all situations. Be a humble, intelligent leader. Know yourself, and help others.

Conclusion

Living an intentional life means taking control. It means planning. It means knowing what you want, where you want to go, and what you want to achieve. However it's also about knowing how to make yourself a better person, both personally and professionally. It's an ongoing, continuous process, and it never ends. That shouldn't be challenging—it should be exciting.

Be a forever learner, always eager to find new knowledge, new ways of doing things, and apply those to your life. Practice humble intelligence, and know yourself. Have someone at all times to watch your blind spots because you can't do it yourself.

Be curious. Be adventurous. Be caring. With the right mentality and the right approach, becoming a better leader is not only possible but easier than you might think. It goes far beyond the boardroom too. It goes into all areas of your life from your spouse to your children to your friends to your acquaintances at church and everyone in between.

Seek to understand, and then seek to be understood.

Acknowledgements

To my amazing wife, Tanna: Without your wisdom, your foundation, and your vision, I would not have had all these great growing experiences to share with others. You truly have helped me navigate life and help me be a better person, husband, dad, and friend. This book was the motivation for me to share the many things it took me a long time to see, but with your help we have had much success. The journey is not done, and I am excited about the future with you in a continued learning and living approach. I look forward to sharing the rest of our lives together and helping whoever we come in contact with. I love you!

To Abby, Allison, and Emily: Thanks for being patient with me as I learned new things about myself and shared them with you. The journey we share from bringing you into this world and helping all three of you navigate each new chapter of your life is something I very much look forward to. Please continue to learn as I learn just as much from you as I do from others. I love all three of you and look forward to your continued growth.

To the old and new Pinnacle team, which has watched me grow in many areas of my life: Thanks for being patient as I worked through many mistakes with an eye on the future.

Thanks to Granger Community Church for providing me and my family with a solid faith-based foundation. This allowed my family and I to take jumps and stretch ourselves outside our comfort zones.

Printed in the United States
By Bookmasters